HOW DO YOU PASS YOUR TIME?

A young English woman's memoir

*of love and life in **Bombay**...*

a million miles away from the Fulham Road

ANNA TURAKHIA

RETHINK PRESS

First published in Great Britain 2017
by Rethink Press (www.rethinkpress.com)

Contents

Prologue

This light story could never have materialised had it not been for my late parents-in-law. They enabled us to have a sheltered but free life, without worries. We were so spoilt that when they were no longer there we were incapable of standing on our own two feet.

Introduction

I was twenty-four when I met my fate; the die was cast, as they say.

I had led a privileged English childhood and being an only child I suppose you could say I was quite indulged.

I loved sport, swimming, riding, skiing. Music was also a passion and I played the piano. I studied ballet till the age of sixteen. Like many little girls, I wanted to be a ballerina, but sadly, at an early stage, I was told I was too tall.

Later, I lived in Switzerland and worked as a governess to a little girl who became my French teacher while I taught her English. Children are the best teachers as they are so patient. Monique would correct my pronunciation and her family would correct my grammar. Once she started school, I started too and took a course in fashion art. It turned out to be a total waste of time and money, My diploma wasn't worth the paper it was written on. On my return to London, I had to be jack of all trades. I studied touch-typing and did office jobs, plus selling in boutiques and hotel receptions.

I was very reliant on my mother and was still living with her in the Fulham Road at the age of twenty-five. One Valentine's Day I was invited to a students' party. There I met Bhupesh and fell in love. I never expected to leave London, and accepting Bhupesh's proposal of marriage and to go and live with him and his extended family in Bombay was something I could never have imagined. I hardly knew where India was. My mother could not afford the time or money to come to the wedding, so there was I, with over five hundred wedding guests and a large new extended family.

The heat, with constant humidity, noise, people, dust and culture is quite extraordinary. People tell me I don't listen; perhaps that's a self-protection mechanism I developed from living in Bombay for nearly thirty years.

Life was good with my children when they were young, but when I had to lose them for nine months of the year whilst they went to boarding school, it wasn't much fun.

My grand-daughter recently wrote a book and consequently my son persuaded me to put pen to paper. "After all, Mummy," he said, "your life story is simply worth telling."

So, I have captured some memories and hope you enjoy them.

Bapuji and a Big Mistake To Start With

Bapuji was an extraordinary self-made man. It seemed he started backwards, as he had to pay off the debts of one of his brothers before making his own fortune. He was a real gentleman. It was a case of the iron hand in the velvet glove. During the period when my husband (then boyfriend) was flying to and from Bombay to London to see me, Bapuji came to London but didn't contact us. I felt at the end of my tether and my mother felt it was her duty to send him a letter, as we had been slighted. You can imagine his surprise on receiving it: as he knew nothing about his dear son's affair! It was a bombshell. My mother didn't mince her words. I never saw her letter but it would have been short and sweet. She ended by saying she thought his behaviour was in the height of bad taste! The cat was out of the bag, so the moment of truth had finally come and the son, not the father, stood in the firing line. Bapuji wanted to know why he had received an upsetting letter from a total stranger.

Years later, when my mother came to India, she was graciously received and she and Bapuji, both book lovers, got on very well. She thought he was charming and he certainly could be. Once, when I had a row with my husband about buying a sari (on this occasion), I said I was not prepared to discuss the matter with an underling, I would go to the higher ranks (his father).

When I went to the office, Bapuji would say, "How did you come? By car? Taxi? I will send the pion (office boy) down with you." Unlike the brothers-in-law, who never asked; for all they cared, I could have come on an elephant.

Bapuji came with me to choose the sari – nothing was too much trouble.

Arrival

The recorded music of "Say a Little Prayer for Me" was playing as I entered the plane.

How appropriate! Off to India, from London to Bombay, to marry an Indian. I was the wrong age – four years his senior – the wrong colour, the wrong religion and a non-vegetarian marrying a vegetarian (not by choice, but by creed, being a Guajarati). What could go wrong?

Anna (aged 29), Bhupesh (aged 25) and my parents in law, Ba and Bapuji. Bombay, c 1965.

The first shock that hits when alighting from the plane is the intense heat that smothers you like a very thick blanket. The second shock on leaving the airport is the noise of the traffic – the constant hooting.

My future parents-in-law came to greet me, so supporting and courteous after the previous longstanding conflict concerning our liaison. The only present conflict now was my hat, which did not meet with the approval of my future husband's mother. "Where did you get that hat?"

Preparation

Another English woman also married to an Indian took me shopping to buy the traditional wedding sari of cream, gold and shocking pink. She pressed me to buy another sari too. According to her, it would appear rude if I just bought the one. It seems the cost of the second was more than my future husband's monthly wage! Help! It was promptly given to my future sister-in-law. No comment.

The Marriage

I had five days to adjust to my new family. I arrived on 9th February and the marriage had to be the 14th, Valentine's Day. The day we had met I had three brothers-in law and four sisters-in-law. The only married brother was Ramesh, the eldest. The youngest was my favourite, much to the concern of his mother. Most Indian brides are professionally made up, professionally coiffed and have the backs of their hands painted. The design is quite a lengthy business called *Mendhi.* The lack of time prevented me from having all this done. The wedding walking around a fire lasted twice as long as normal as the holy man insisted on translating everything he said, for my benefit. We didn't have a reception as it would have been very costly and time-consuming.

The wedding: Bhupesh and Anna's marriage. Bombay 1963

The Honeymoon

We were whisked away to Mysore, South India, to a majestic hotel, The Krishna Raja Saga, which had beautiful gardens and fountains that lit up at night. It was grand and, much like the spider in our bathroom, it frightened the pair of us!

Settling In

B a means "mother" in Guajarati, and as Ba lived about ten minutes away from us, I would frequently visit her. We did not speak each other's language, but had no problems communicating. She was religious, and on my first visit I joined her in prayer. After that I used to wait until she had finished praying. Bapuji ("father" in Guajarati) asked Ba what we discussed, and my husband asked me. Our stories were the same. Who said language is a problem?

On The Move

We started our life together in a bungalow in Kandivlee, a suburb near my husband's factory, the family business. He was in plastics: wholesale containers, spectacle frames, umbrella handles and ping-pong balls. I was not popular as I went around with the kitchen scissors freeing donkeys by cutting the rope around their neck which was attached to one leg. When I went to buy vegetables and fruit a crowd would follow me. We were in the sticks;I it wasn't a European location like Bombay so they weren't used to Europeans.

Once, while hanging out the clothes, I had another audience. Suddenly, I stopped and threw a bucket of water over them, which shocked me more than it shocked them. At another time there was a strike at the factory and posters were put up with rude things written about the family.

A Little Bit Of What You Fancy

Juhu is a beach resort, westernised, unlike Kandivlee. There was the sweetest vacant flat on the ground floor) in a house with one flat upstairs and one downstairs, on each side. I loved it, but my husband said it was too expensive for us. My dear Bapuji said that if I liked it I could have it, and I liked it!

Our new neighbours were great. Above us, an Air India pilot who serenaded his wife by singing below her balcony. Next door on the ground floor was a holiday home owned by a Delhi family, and upstairs lived a film star, Feroz. Opposite was a tailor who would flatten Feroz's tyres from time to time. Feroz knew who the culprit was, but felt his arms were tied as she was a woman. Our dog also disliked film stars and went upstairs to do his business on Feroz's front mat.

Trouble In Paradise

There are two big things in India: cricket and film stars, not necessarily in that order. But not everyone is star struck. We had two great hotels nearby, Juhu Hotel (a family hotel) and the Sun-n-Sand (modern and glamorous, with a pool). Their little bar was our local too, and one night we and all our neighbours sat there together. Feroz's younger brother, Ahmed, went to the men's cloakroom, where he was insulted, unbeknownst to us.

When we left, two men were waiting for us at the entrance. It all kiced off. The hotel tried to help us by closing the gates to keep us apart from our attackers, but they were waiting by our home. There was a gorgeous bust-up – I love a good fight. My husband called for the police, not that our hero needed any help!

Something To Remember

Feroz had arranged to meet me on the beach. He had booked two horses and we went for a canter along the sand – it was like something out of a film. As I told you, I was very star minded (more Barbara Cartland minded really!). My husband sometimes fancied himself as a star too. On another occasion, upon leaving Sun-n-Sand, he lay on top of the car and burst into song, true Bollywood style. Suddenly, my husband's younger brother passed by – whoops! He was not amused. Being a little shy I guess he had not considered one of the dangers of visiting Juhu, a Bombay suburb, was that he could meet his mad brother.

As Strong As An Ox

My husband did not only believe in his dancing abilities, but imagined he had superhuman strength. Once, on the road, a bullock cart passed by too closely and Superman thought he could stop it with one arm. Needless to say, the bullock continued forward regardless of my husband's moans and groans. He shouted that his arm was broken, but as he was always so dramamtic I didn't believe him. To humour him, we went to a doctor who confirmed his statement. The doctor asked how it had happened – we did not tell him the truth, as he would not have believed us.

An ox eating some of our garden

A coconut tree climber

Never Slow Down

We had another adventure on the road which was not our fault. It happened when we were still in Kandivlee, returning from Bombay very late at night. We were conned into stopping, an old trick, by a girl struggling on a bike who looked in need of help. We stopped on the remote road and suddenly two chaps appeared from nowhere. One pulled my husband's shirt and I was incensed when the buttons began falling off, so I reached over and punched him. My husband accelerated fast. I was pregnant which forced us to move quickly.

It was a close call. Warning: never slow down on a deserted road in India. As we should have known that, perhaps it was our fault.

Daily Chores

Our daily help Mary introduced us to Hilary, her husband, who was a fantastic cook. He worked part-time at the family's factory. Once you sampled his cooking, you were hooked. He came every evening.

I must explain about the complicated daily chores and why help was needed. The water must be boiled and filtered daily, which takes forever. Everything in the kitchen must be in airtight containers, or the shelves would be crawling with ants. There are also regular visits by pest control to chase the cockroaches into the next door flat. They then return promptly when they undergo the same procedure there. Dust is everywhere on account of the open dirt roads.

The amount of washing is mind-boggling because of the heat. As an example, my husband showered and changed three times daily. I always remember the first time my mother saw our daily wash. She could not believe it. It was more than a normal month's washing in England.

In And Out of Prison

We'll return to our cook, Hilary. Mary, his wife, came in crying, saying he had been accused of stealing. I needed to speak to my eldest brother-in-law, Ramesh, who was such an over-powering person that I always felt stupid in his presence, and probably made him think I was too. I thought it was better to go and see him in person not phone – so I did.

I stormed past his secretary who tried to stop me (there were business associates in the office) and made my dramatic entrance.

"If Hilary is guilty, then the whole of the factory is – you might as well put them all in prison!" I shouted.

Ramesh knew better than to argue with a woman's logic. He apologised profusely and telephoned the prison, ordering them to release Hilary immediately. Prisons in India are not like they are here; there, prisoners are beaten unmercifully.

It didn't end there for me, though. My husband had been out of Bombay on business and when he found out what had happened he went mad.

"Don't you ever go to the factory again! You will be forbidden in the future."

I don't miss it.

Sweet Innocence

My daughter was born in 1964. She was named Peshna. "Pesh" from Bhupesh, my husband's name, and "na" from Anna. Peshna was a beautiful baby. The first time my baby girl saw a flower was magic. Her look of love and amazement made me realise how we adults take everything for granted, so blind to the beauty around us. She put out her little hand and touched it so gently. Precious memories like that help us face the less agreeable ones in the future.

Sweet innocence: Wiggy in her cot, 1964

Weddings

To my shame, I never learned to speak Hindi – the trouble was everyone spoke English in Bombay – but I loved Indian films, with their dancing and jewellery. My favourite film star was Dilip Kumar; I had a few pictures of him around the sitting room, much to Bapuji's amusement. He often came to see his little granddaughter with exciting invitations to weddings. Indians are contantly invited to the weddings of all their business associates.

They were an obligatory business function for him, but she was always so excited as I helped her put on her party dress. They were both so happy to be together. *Don't let go of Grandpa's hand,* were my strict orders. There are so many guests at Indian weddings, she would have been terrified had she found herself alone. Five ice creams later, she would return.

Weddings: Anna and Wiggy (Peshna)
aged two-and-a-half at Bhupesh's brother's wedding

Weddings: A kiss from Ba, Peshna's Indian grandmother

Wiggy And Grandma

Wiggy and Grandma: Wiggy and Grandma
at Sun-n-Sand Hotel, Juhu 1967

I nicknamed Peshna "Wiggy": she waddled when she walked! Ba picked up on it and walked behind her, moving her hips from side to side. My mother visited us many times; throughout her first visit, Wiggy's face would light up when she saw her in the morning, greeting her with a "Hello Danma". You would think the Queen of England had just arrived. She certainly had a royal reception!

Spontaneous Nights

One night we went to the Sun-n-Sand for a meal and saw Ahmed, Feroz's brother. There was a young blonde eating alone and Ahmed asked the waiter to find out if she was waiting for someone. She was alone and accepted Ahmed's invitation to join him.

We all ended up going to the Juhu company's bungalow. Putting on some recorded music, my husband decided to show Ahmed a film audition and started dancing around invisible trees waving my scarf. Ahmed was most impressed and thought he was real film material.

Let's Fly Away

On one of my trips to London, I went to Harley Street to have a course of injections for my varicose veins. The surgeon had been in India and was very interested to know if the English people mixed with me, as I was married to an Indian. "Well no," I replied, "but I don't want to mix with them." Times change and standards drop. "Oh – it's like that now, is it?" he said.

Little Children

Once we were in an air-conditioned coach, and some little children in rags waved and smiled at us. Had I been in their shoes – correction: what shoes? – had I been in their *place*, I wouldn't have felt so friendly.

People think they are dirty but their mothers wash them daily by throwing a bucket of water over their heads, despite their tears. Their clothes are washed and, without a clothes line, they are put on the pavement to dry. Not the cleanest solution, but their only one.

Servants

We had so many different servants. My husband told me they were taking advantage of my kindness. I told him I knew, but I was not prepared to change my nature for them. He understood. Indians can be very disrespectful of their servants, almost as if they are a lower caste. I just used to treat them with respect like proper human beings, not doormats. Many servants had to sleep outside the front door on a mat. I was extraordinary by simply treating them with respect.

They had never been considered, so when they were, they thought it a sign of weakness where they could take full advantage. In all, they didn't know what consideration was.

A Bundle Of Joy

When I first saw my son, I screamed – much to the distress of The Holy Family Hospital staff. Then, when I arrived home, my daughter screamed and covered her ears as she ran to hide. He never stopped crying, day or night until he was mobile, then he was at peace with the world.

Gloria, a Swiss woman whose husband had known mine since their college days, asked me whether I was going to call my son Buan – the first two syllables of Bhupesh and Anna. This custom was well established at the time. With the last two letters reversed, Peshan is an Icelandic boy's name. We called our son Keran, not Kieran or Kevin, just something different.

The second two syllables of our names made up my daughter's name, Peshna. Names usually mean something in India. A lady in the swimming pool asked me what Peshna meant and I said Peach Blossom!

A bundle of joy: Anna's mother, Grandma,
holding baby Keran, 1966

Kailash: Our Flat

We moved to our flat in Bombay in 1970. It was not part of a skyscraper, happily; the building only had six floors. We were on the first floor and the Israeli Consulate was on the fourth. People were most impressed seeing an armed guard outside our building. I told them he was there for my protection.

The truth is he killed himself after a few years of sheer boredom.

Grandma, Peshna and Keran, with Fatso our dog and
Tina's bottom! In Kailash, Bombay 1974

Hairdresser Gossip

My hairdresser in Bombay was grumbling about the attitude of westerners in India, and I told her that they, the Indians, were partly to blame, Many Indians kowtowed to foreigners, so the foreigners took full advantage of it.

They come on a two-year contract and suddenly they have a domestic cook, driver, gardener, dhobi (washing and ironing man), ayah (nanny) included with the firm's flat. Foreigners are not used to this and they become what is described as "ex-pats". Quite snooty and more "God save the gracious Queen" than they were at home. I found this quite fake and not an authentic lifestyle, and could not really empathise with it.

Even the servants became snooty. When we interviewed some servants they did not want to work for us when they found out that my husband was not European but an Indian. In fact my maidservant Annie used to tell me the reason she had taken so long to get meat from the butcher was because the butcher served all the fully foreign housekeepers first!

Foreign nationality and white skin were status symbols in Bombay. Foreigners were always wanted at Indian weddings, to appear in the pictures and make the function have more importance.

Foreigners First

My little home help, Annie, was Goan and once she took so long on a trip to a local shop I had to ask her what had happened. She said, "What to tell you, Madam?" She never called me the usual Memsahib. Every time a foreigner came in the shop, they were served first. The assistant was Goan too, so I asked why she didn't say something in Goan to him. She should have.

Exception To The Rule

I once went to a vegetable and fruit stall to buy some oranges and the stall holder said, "Would you mind going to the stall next door?" I wasn't offended. He wasn't rude and he must have had some very bad experiences with westerners previously. In fact, I admired him.

Why do foreigners have to misbehave abroad? My grandmother used to say, "Once the dustbin rises, it smells." I think that sums it up!

Charity

I used to visit a hospital with children of different religions and languages. They had, as they say now, learning difficulties. I would go on my own back – no organisation.

I took sweets, balloons and plastic beads from my husband (they loved making necklaces), though they never had them the following week, as a family member or staff would take them.

An English group had a box of toys that was kept locked. It was opened for one hour and then locked again. I used to do miming for them, pretending I was drunk. They found that very funny.

Another thing I would do was with my mother on Christmas Eve, when we would wrap up small gifts with "Boy" or "Girl" written on them. It took a good half a day. They were bought with my husband's money, no so-called charity organisation.

On our way to dinner, we dropped the bag of presents off at a luxurious block of flats. We were invited into the sitting room, where a massive Christmas tree dominated the room. With a "thank you" we were shown the door – not even offered a sherry. We would have declined anyway, as my husband was waiting in the car, so they would have been perfectly safe! They say charity starts at home. If it starts, however, it isn't always so sweet.

Say It With Flowers

Dilip Kumar, my favourite film star, was having a coffee in the Sea Lounge Taj Hotel. Wiggy was about three years old at the time. We popped downstairs and bought a rose, which my daughter presented to him on our return. Some things are not rehearsed.

An Incident

We will not be moved. As Margaret Thatcher said, "The lady is not for turning" – and my husband held the same view. One evening in Juhu, my husband decided to sit on the floor near our daughter's cot. My mother was in the sitting room reading the newspaper. All was at peace, for a short spell! I decided to force him to move – a big mistake as he did not take orders very well. I pushed, I shoved until I had to stop for a rest. Then I started all over again.

It was exhausting – like trying to move a mountain! After following this procedure several times, I finally gave in. Totally exhausted, I lay on the bed. Slowly the mountain rose and moved out of the room while my mother continued to read her paper!

Wiggy's First Word

My daughter's first word wasn't "Mama" but "Baboo". He was our swabber man and came daily to clean the floors. Every day he would say, "Baboo, Baboo" as he went into the bathroom, so one day Wiggy said it back and he was delighted.

Our Neighbour's Dog

Our neighbour's dog, a Labrador (Orm, if I remember correctly), took a shine to us and felt it his duty to guard us when we went to the beach, so we were never worried about beggars and hawkers.

No one came near. One afternoon my husband wanted to say hello on his way back from the factory. I warned him not to come too close – so we talked from a distance!

Paint

I made the children's room very pretty; I painted a rabbit on their white cupboard and the front of a house on their chest of drawers. I painted some nursery rhymes on the walls. The place was suddenly very quiet, too quiet. Hilary came in, following black oil paint footprints. Wiggy was covered in black – not easily removed!

Bedtime Stories

I had made a tape (I remember we had this old Grundig tape recorder) with my *The Cat in the Hat* story, and songs like "Sing a Song of Sixpence" and "Twinkle, Twinkle Little Star". Bapuji knew that one.

Peshna's bedroom in Juhu, Bombay, 1965

When we had friends around I would put on the tape and the children were asleep long before the end.

Grandparents can have such a close bond with their grandchildren, can't they? They are really so important and so necessary for each other.

Whisky A Go-Go

When I arrived in India there was prohibition. This meant only foreigners and British passport holders could get a drink by producing their permit, which entitled you to a certain amount of units per month. We didn't bother to apply for a permit for ages, until friends persuaded us to change our ways and join them wining and dining, which started in a bar.

Bhupesh having a drink in the Cricket Club of India

After that it was a one-way street. Every outing started with whisky. I can't remember how long the prohibition lasted, but when it was over we drank every evening at home.

At 7.30pm, out came the trolley and we drank until our late dinner. My mother wasn't a whisky drinker. She preferred a gin and tonic – or should I say gins and tonics. My daughter thought we should half fill the gin bottle with water as gin is colourless, so every evening my mother would have her gin and water with tonic and ice. She was convinced the drink suppliers were watering it down because it had no taste, she told us.

Our dog, Tina, was very partial to a small gin and tonic on the odd occasion, much to the annoyance of my husband. All the parties we attended had whisky flowing like water. I remember deciding to drink cokes one night and I was nearly hysterical at the end of the evening. The conversation of a load of drunks is so repetitive that it can drive you mad. If you can't fight them, join them, as the saying goes. It is so hard to be sober among drinkers.

Friends

When you think about old friends, you often wonder how you met them and sometimes recall the strange way it all began. The friends who persuaded us to get a drink permit were in the Natraj Hotel dancing and there was a singer (the cabaret). Joan, Dev's English wife, wanted to dance and Bhupesh, my husband, wanted to dance, so the two danced, much to the annoyance of the cabaret. That was the start of our friendship.

Before we met them, I was convinced we were the only mixed couple in India!

Joan De'Mello was an Air India air hostess who was then a ground hostess working in the Sun-n-Sand at a desk in the lobby. We became friends as we were neighbours in Juhu. Her late Indian husband had been a steward for Air India. She had a daughter who was only three years old at the time.

Then there was Mr Soman, Chief Inspector of Police. We met at a reception somewhere. He and his family would often join us in Juhu for lunch on a Sunday, along with

Joan. We all got on so well and spent many weekends laughing.

Dr Narula was a mistake! Narula is quite a common name, it seems; my husband was trying to contact an old friend and the wrong Narula showed up, which started another friendship – need I go on? They say friends come and go. I don't know about the go part. They certainly came – and stayed, which was great.

I had another friend called Inez. She had a hairdresser's in Bandra almost next to where Pat sold children's clothes – authentic Indian styles alongside classic western ones. I haven't much patience with tailors, so this was very handy. It is all so complicated getting the material and choosing a pattern, and it is never ready when they say it will be.

Bandra was our nearest shopping centre, very near Juhu.

Talking of fashion, my dear husband was always a law unto himself. He always wore his trousers on his hips like they do nowadays. Strange to think of him as a secret fashion icon!

Not For Me

At one point, my husband's company owned a Mercedes. Feroz, our neighbour, asked Keran if he would like a ride in his jeep.

"No thank you," came the retort, "I'm in the Mercedes and you are only in a jeep!"

When he offered my daughter and me a lift to Bombay, Feroz received a much warmer response. She was thrilled to be sitting in the front seat, seeing passers-by recognising the film star next to her. Feroz treated her like a little princess and opened the door for her on our arrival. A perfect day. The earth moved, as they say.

Noisy Nights

It did once shake during the middle of the night when we had a small tremor. It was like a massive groan. We ran outside and the next morning one could see quite a few cracks.

Weddings Again

Feroz had a beautiful sister called Dilu and she would come into our small garden on her way up to her brother's. She loved the children. We were invited to her wedding held at the Taj Hotel. The children were delighted. Like A Little Princess and Little Lord Fontleroy!

My two nephews and their wives: Baumik and Seema, Alpa and Sanjay, and my son Keran.

Crystal (Queenie's daughter) and Manu's wedding, 1989

Pearl dancing with Dad, Queenie's husband, at her wedding

Bobo dancing at Crystal's wedding

We attended another very beautiful wedding, for my brother-in-law. It was held at the race course grounds. Coloured fairy lights covered the trees. Light western music played in the background with a sumptuous buffet to tempting our taste buds. As the grounds were so big, it wasn't at all crowded.

Bhupesh and Anna at Crystal's wedding, 1989

Tina

Our flat in Bombay had an underground car park with a watchman who, rather suddenly, acquired a dachshund. It seemed that one of the flat owners gave her to him. Aren't people strange – he could hardly afford to keep himself, let alone a dog. The poor little thing would be tied up down there day and night. We offered to have her, much to his relief. That was the start of Tina.

Originally, dachshunds were the one breed of dog I didn't like, but the family I lived with in Switzerland had one and to know one is to love one. So, Tina had the little basket in the hall. We also had two guinea pigs on the balcony, two birds and a terrapin. When Tina was naughty, I would put her basket outside the front door. That was the biggest punishment as her home was her basket. I would peep at her through the letterbox. She would sit there with her head down looking very sorry for herself.

The watchman would ring the doorbell as he was worried about her. People step over a body on the pavement without concern, but money talks. Tina was a rich little dog who needed help!

As we only lived on the first floor my husband thought we could let Tina out alone. Big mistake, as we later learned when we noticed a very fat tummy. "Shame on you," I told her, "bringing shame to the family."

The outcome of this little adventure ended with nine puppies. Where would I put them? I couldn't put them in the hall where Tina used to sleep. It was not peaceful enough for her. Fortunately, we had the balcony. Unlike normal balconies with steel railings, we had a long balcony with a wall so it was a safe place for them. Tina's basket was moved there. When we opened the balcony door to the sitting room they would make a beeline for the kitchen. It must have smelt of food. The leader, probably Fatso, found a piece of bread and was followed by his eight siblings.

We had a sofa on one side of the sitting room and opposite a mattress with a fitted cover and bolsters. They loved that and had a real job trying to get over the bolsters.

They soon lost interest in their mum's milk when presented with sardines and bread.

Hill Stations

We used to go to London every two years and each year between the London visits we went to Marbleshwar, an Indian hill station near Bombay. The three nephews would come, which made five children and one dog. Our driver seemed alright – until I realised he was an alcoholic.

I sacked him and if I had then taken the car out, it would have been our final ride. Unbeknown to us, he had, in revenge, drained the oil and cut the brakes. Imagine driving in the hills with their dangerous hair pin bends and narrow ghat roads with five children in a car with no brakes. I did not have a driving license and that was what saved us, despite my eldest nephew, Rajesh, nagging me to take them out the car. Our hotel was great, a lot of bungalows in a row – perfect for the families and pets who were served before us!

Our neighbours were Goan and would sit on their balcony having a drink before lunch. Keran was about three and as he carefully parked his tricycle, they shouted to invite him for a drink.

Off he would go for his lemonade and dash of beer every day. He thought he was very grown up. Once, Rajesh, the eldest nephew, returned from his vegetarian restaurant and asked about Keran's whereabouts. I told him he was having a drink before lunch with our neighbours. He couldn't believe it, seeing empty beer bottles in full view. We would go down to the lake, have chips and ketchup and take a rowing boat out. Once, our dog jumped in, climbed back into the boat and shook himself all over us. There was never a dull moment, not even a dry one!

Cousins. From left to the right: Rajesh, Hitesh, Wiggy, Sanjay and Keran in Mabeleshwar Hill station, 1968

Wiggy in a rowing boat with Rajesh, her cousin,
a friend and Bhupesh sitting at the back. 1968

Bhupesh

Anna

Monkey Business

Hill stations have many monkeys and Marbeleshwar is no exception. On one of our walks we were alone, until a very aggressive male monkey jumped out on us. Annie, our little helper, screamed and fell over, which attracted our male intruder. Seeing Annie on the ground, he decided to claim her for his own and wanted to carry her off to his den. Keran started to cry and I stood there transfixed – it all happened so fast. The only one who acted quickly was my daughter, who picked up a stone and frightened him off.

We quickly returned and other holiday makers made us feel safe again. Who knows what lies behind the bushes.

The London Holidays

The children called London "The air-conditioned capital".

On one occasion, my mother rented a chauffeur-driven Hertz to collect us from the airport. I'm sure she had as much (or more) pleasure than we did. There was always a spread fit for a king awaiting us.

The "to do" things were to go on the buses, up and down escalators and spend forever in Hamleys Toy Shop in Regent Street. Each floor was different: one dolls, another trains, and so on. They say it's the best toy store in the world.

There was fun in waiting for the milk man, who not only delivered milk with cream on top but other groceries, even chocolate digestive biscuits. They loved Swiss, Belgian and English chocolate. , but not least, was the English TV, as in Bombay television was in its very early stages.

The children's TV programmes! *Skippy the Bush Kangaroo*, *The Magic Roundabout*, *Blue Peter*, *Noddy*... In the early evening, my daughter had *Dusty Springfield*, weekly, fun shows like *Love Thy Neighbour* and *Top of the Pops* on Thursdays.

But had you asked if they preferred cream teas or feeding the ducks, the ducks would have won hands down. Around the corner was our beautiful Battersea Park where an ice cream man stood at the entrance. "One only," I would say, "going in or going out." A family of ducks would follow our boat on the boating lake.

One year, my husband asked my mother to hire a flat for our upcoming holiday in London, as her home was a bit small for all of us to live in comfortably.

She rented a garden flat (a basement) in Holland Park. It was so beautiful. One massive room, divided by a screen when wanted. A double bed that came out of the wall. A small bed, a roomy yellow bathroom and a blue and white kitchen with a phone on the wall (very new then). There were baskets of geraniums leading to the front door and Holland Park itself was nearby.

Stars

I loved film stars and went to the cinema weekly with Glin, the super swimmer. Neither of us understand Hindi but enjoyed the dancing and music, beautiful colours and jewellery. As we were coming out of the Oberoi Hotel, Jeetendra, an Indian star, was leaving the bar. I was the only one who recognised him. His Lordship and our two friends hadn't any idea who he was, although I was the foreigner among them. He looked just the same as he did on screen. He wasn't one of my favourites – it was Annie, our nanny, who liked him.

Dharamendra was mine (if only). I had just dropped the children off at the airport on their way to boarding school as he passed by me – I immediately forgot the children.

Shashi was very popular as he was so good looking. my mother would go all starry-eyed. He introduced himself to me in the Sun-n-Sand Hotel pool. I knew who he was; I knew his wife.

He came over with his daughter to see Tina's litter – all nine of them! Sometime later, on another occasion, he came to collect his daughter who had been watching Charlie Chaplin on my baby projector.

Once, Cliff Richard visited India. It was a Saturday and I was with my female friends in Breach Candy swimming pool bar. Joan suddenly said, "Isn't that Cliff Richard down there?". It was, and I forced his hostess to introduce me to him. He gave a concert before leaving and we eight ladies attended it.

Keran with Shashi Kapoor, a famous Indian
film star and Felicity Kendal's brother-in-law

Schools

Schools can be fun or a nightmare. We had the experience of both.

Junior Cathedral School in Bombay wasn't a happy experience for my daughter. Picking her up one morning, I was temporarily flattered as all the children seemed to know who I was.

"Well," my daughter said, "all the children have a mother – but not all have a dog!"

Dear Tina, our bag of mischief dog who behaved like a proper *memsahib*. For your ears only, Tina's boyfriends led to her having an abortion and a hysterectomy.

Middle school was much better, but my daughter wanted to go to boarding

school. One evening, in the bar at Breach Candy swimming pool, our troubled conversation was overheard by two ladies. One worked in the British High Commission and her children had been to Hebron, a mainly missionary school that accepted non-missionary children too.

The staff were from England, Australia, Canada and all over the world. They usually came over to teach on two-year contracts.

We had seen a few boarding schools which were pretty grim, more like prisons, but Hebron Junior School, Coonoor, and the senior school at Ooty were two idyllic schools in the Nilgiri Hills in Tamil Nadu, South India. Children were able to take their British G.C.E's there.

We decided to send both our daughter and son there. Keran was only seven, but I told him that if he didn't like it after the first term he could return to Bombay. He hated the first term but I pressed him not to judge. When he returned for the second term he loved it. Before starting boarding school, Keran had tried ballet dancing like his sister. I didn't tell my dear husband and let it die a natural death. He then learned to play the piano, also like his sister, and that continued at boarding school. Later, his piano teacher would give a little annual concert and Shashi Kapoor (the film star)'s boys who played the piano were there too. I was sitting behind the boys and overheard their conversation.

Keran said, "Do you do ballet?" The boys replied "No!" with an odd look. "Oh, you should," Keran continued, "you don't know what you are missing.".

I must tell you about Janine, a French lady who lived in a slum near their boarding school in Coonoor. The children would pass her house whilst walking to church every Sunday. I went to visit her. She was so sweet and still had a strong French accent. She had two dogs, one a French poodle called Fifi. How French can you get?!

She was very poor and lived in a little, brick one-room home. She invited me to tea. There was a lace cloth on an orange box, with a teapot that had a chipped spout. We had matching cups. Her husband was a driver. Her family, needless to say, had disowned her when she married her Indian boyfriend. We looked at many old photographs of her and her family, taken when she was young in Panchgani.

I met her many times and on one occasion I took her to the Ritz Hotel for tea. She was so excited and, not being used to makeup, she put on her rouge in the two little blocks, making her look like a China doll.

The children were mystified by our friendship, to put it mildly. I told them that I would rather have tea off an orange box with a lady than tea in a mansion with a vulgar individual.

Keran and Peshna having a pony ride, 1974

Parties And Dances

The Swiss were always having parties, for children as well as adults, so my dual nationality was a great help. They had Easter and Christmas parties for children and many dinner dances for us. I had a French coffee party every fortnight with friends, European and Indian, all French-speaking. We took it in turns to host the party in our homes. We all put on a super spread, savoury and sweet, and couldn't have eaten lunch after our snacks!

On one occasion a rather shabby Englishman came to collect his wife and the maid announced that her driver was waiting.

My greatest friend, Queenie, was a hotel manageress. Queenie and her friends, Janet who was in the printing business, and Gunie a housewife, and I would meet monthly for lunch. Sometimes at the Shalimar Hotel where Queenie worked or the CCI, the Cricket Club of India, where Gunie and I were members. You could eat in the bar, the main restaurant or the Chinese restaurant. There was such a choice of food and all the food was excellent, but we would have laughed just as much without the lavish cuisine. We never stopped laughing like silly teenagers every time. I don't know what got into us, I was laughing before I met them.

The CCI held Christmas and New Year dances in the large grounds. There was a restaurant called the Volga in Kala Ghoda (Black Horse) which gave Sunday tea dances too. Another nice restaurant in the same district was called the The Bullock Cart. It was a great little place with a very small dance floor (glass with coloured lights underneath) and good food. If you just wanted to dance you sat in another area and had a coffee or another drink – ideal for youngsters who couldn't afford a dinner.

It was casual, so you could go in jeans or dressed up to the nines. No one took any notice. Queenie often had friends at the hotel for lunch. We would have a vacant room which made it nice and private. She also arranged parties at the Sun-n-Sand Hotel, which may have been partly owned by her Shalimar Hotel boss. There was dancing by the light of the silvery moon, as they say, at the side of the swimming pool. The Shalimar did dinner dances with a small dance floor and matching band. Many restaurants had dancing then: Breach Candy sometimes had dances, but they didn't last very long as the flats overlooking the pool complained about the noise. At the last dance we attended, His Lordship complained about my partner who picked me up and I was suddenly higher than everyone else. I can assure you, it was as much a shock to me as it was to the other dancers. I was in disgrace for the rest of the evening – from then on, dancing was out.

We went to a great party in the suburbs. The hosts were Germans and all the little bungalows were around the pool. We were terribly late as it took us ages to find them. When we got there at long last, they were really pleased to see us and we had a great time despite my tactlessly remarking, "Oh, it's so English" when they would have probably preferred "Cosmopolitan" or, indeed, "German".

We gave many parties and Nancy, an Irish neighbour, always came with her ice bucket on our request. Her husband wasn't a dancer and preferred reading a good book. We always had a mixed bunch for events that had nothing to do with business, birthdays or anniversaries. We didn't need an excuse, which was why most people gave parties. "What's the occasion?" we were always asked. They couldn't understand why there wasn't one as a reason for our party.

A German couple we knew, Margaret and Anu, would not attend any parties except ours. He felt at home and used to do exactly what he wanted, which was throwing a ball down our very long hall to the dog.

We had three shelves that extended from the balcony wall and formed a long table to display our cold buffet. I always had cold food so the non-drinkers didn't have to wait until 10.30pm or later to eat. If we gave a cocktail party, we would hire a waiter from the swimming pool bar to serve drinks and snacks.

A Swiss party in Bombay

One great advantage in India is you never get angry neighbours on account of the noise. Glin, the young swimmer who went to Hindi films with me and joined the daily morning dog walks, would also come. Our parties were the only ones she was allowed to attend alone. She was only twenty-one at the time and although we were mad, her parents trusted us. I remember one couple: the husband would mime a stripper to music. He never took anything off and it was so clever and funny. My husband was a bit uncomfortable with the whole act.

An English cockney couple who loved dancing and were very good, were frequent guests. Ramesh Patel, a college friend from the past, would also attend. He would only dance when he was drunk, then the next morning he would tell us he didn't dance. Joan, a school head teacher, and her husband who was in textiles used to come, and our other Joan, from Juhu, and Dr Narula, who lived on the same road, also came to our parties. The last of our regular friends were the Austins. He was English and his wife Assamese. They had two girls, our children's school friends.

Bhupesh playing a Bollywood star

Anna at a Swiss dinner party, Oberoi Hotel, 1971

Clubs

India offers heat, servants and clubs. None of these appeal to me. I'm not a sun worshipper, I find a servant very intrusive and I dislike clubs. Some help, though is a necessary evil with the excessive heat and clubs were much cheaper than restaurants when you were treating a guest to a meal. There are many clubs in Bombay and just a few elite ones: The Wellington Golf Club, Breach Candy swimming baths, Cricket Club of India with a swimming pool, tennis, table tennis, squash and billiards, along with several restaurants.

Wiggy in Breach Candy swimming pool, Bombay, 1972

Our little French coffee parties could have been termed as our private club. All the members, apart from a French teacher and yours truly, had a cook and a boy who served the snacks in white gloves and arrived when the bell rung. It's hard to imagine, isn't it?! The Indian ladies are usually members of 'kittie parties'! This is not a hen party like in England, where everyone gets wasted, but a very mouth-watering private lunch or in a smart restaurant.

Cars And The Driving Test

I remember looking at our car keys hanging on the hall wall. Our driver was away and I thought I must learn to drive. Our friend said he would pay for my licence, as it wasn't worth taking the test with the inconvenience and the heat. I was mystified and thought the whole idea very dishonest so I decided to go ahead and participated in the farce it turned out to be.

I was in the car with others for the test. When it was my turn at the wheel, I didn't move. In spite of this, I was given a licence. I couldn't believe it. It seems that if you fail they are obliged to give you another course free of charge, which they want to avoid at all costs.

I didn't drive as I knew I couldn't and found a teacher through a friend, who taught me in my own car. He would come on his scooter every day. I would shake when I heard him arrive; he was strict. Our driver walked out. Sahib wasn't pleased and he blamed me. I didn't want his job, I just thought it made sense not to be dependent on him. I was taught to drive in my company car - a red Fiat that I called Noel. When

Keran and I would wash the car we always had an audience.

Keran was quite small but loved helping. Can you imagine, a woman washing a car, and not only a woman, but a white woman – unheard of!

The brakes failed on two occasions. Once in mid-traffic, and I managed to park it near a church in the suburbs, much to the annoyance of my husband. Another time, I was going down the hill on our road. Help! I was trying to indicate to all and sundry to get out of the way – and happily it ended without an accident.

Another breakdown was with Keran when he was about eight-years-old. The car failed, and turned towards the swimming pool. I told Keran to steer and I pushed. In India, in this situation, only a beggar would help; a middle-class man wouldn't dream of it, it's too menial. Suddenly three Australians left the pool and came to our help. When I told my friend, she said, "Anna, have you been reading Barbara Cartland again?"

My daughter reminded me about our car trips to her aunts, my husband's three sisters. They all lived in the suburbs and the traffic was chaotic. The roads, often muddy lanes, were not only full of cars but rickshaws, bullock carts, bicycles and hand carts pulled by men or even women. The noise was unbearable, with constant hooting behind cars waiting at the lights. People crossing everywhere and there were no zebra crossings. Not that the Indian pedestrians would have adhered to a rule like a zebra crossing. How I managed to drive through Bombay I will never know. It's not something an average Indian would have dreamed of considering.

Dogs

After Tina had her litter of nine – "nearly a football team" as Bapuji said – we kept two, Tommy and Fatso, who was fat and the biggest. The name stuck. Tommy had beautiful eyes and long lashes. He was fully black and those soft eyes could deceive you. He fancied Glin the swimmer, and would whine after dropping her home on the way back from the race course. We were the ones who felt like crying with the smell of poo after they had rolled in it. It was necessary to hit the shower. Tina didn't mind, nor did Fatso, but Tommy just cried. One day, Tommy and Fatso started to fight in the kitchen. It was really vicious. Poor Mona, our dhobi man, was trying to do the ironing.

Tommy was small boned, he used his head and was very sly, whereas Fatso was like a bull in a China shop – no strategy. My money would always have been on Tommy. I picked up one by the back of the neck as they would have fought to the death. They had to be separated and we had a week keeping them apart before we could get rid of one of them. Then a lady whose mother had lost her dog wanted Tommy to be her mother's birthday present. She brought him to visit us. He had a red halter that suited his shiny black coat and long eyelashes.

Sanjay, my nephew, came over. He was usually with us as he was nearer the ages of our two than his own brothers. We went to Worli Sea Face, where they would take turns on a skateboard being pulled by Fatso, who loved it. It was so funny as he was unpredictable he would suddenly stop. The perfect Bombay driver: no warning signs, full speed ahead.

I had to unlearn driving once settled in the UK, as I had been taught in India. My teacher would shout and her dog would growl on the back seat.

Dogs have a sixth sense. One evening, alone in our sitting room, I was thinking about my daughter and felt the full impact of her loss. Tina got out of her basket and sat by my side. It made things worse. I went to the bedroom and sat on the floor by our bed. I sobbed my heart out and Tina yelped and yelped. Not a howl, a yelp as if she had been beaten. My neighbour, Janet, would wisely comment on the subject of children: "When they are young they hurt your arms and when they are older they hurt your heart."

Some Indians risk being run over to avoid touching a dog. They will step off the pavement to avoid the contact of a dog. They feel compelled to have a shower as soon as possible if they have touched a dog.

Indian dog lovers usually have pedigree dogs – it's a status thing. I remember when I found this little puppy on the road long after I had left Kailash. I kept him, of course. It was dangerous; unbeknownst to me he had been bitten by a rat. I washed his bite with disinfectant and slowly his fur grew over the little bald area and all was well. I started a new trend in Bombay as I started to notice other dog owners owning mongrels and not just pedigrees.

More Friends

Talking about dogs, I made a friend in Kailash through a dog. She was an English lady living with her son and family. Her dog Blackie was a mongrel; Fatso and Blackie were arch enemies. They lived on the floor above us and Blackie would growl outside our door. I told The Master I was going to see her about Blackie. Her son opened the door; he was charming and invited me in for a drink, so that was the end of the problem – and the beginning of our friendship.

Sanjay Bagchi, a textile commissioner, must have met us at a cocktail party. One evening after we had been meeting regularly he came round without his wife. I was in the bedroom and my husband announced that my boyfriend had arrived. "Which one"? I asked. I thought I would teach him a lesson and make him eat his words. I gave Sanjay a kiss on the cheek, explaining my behaviour. He went along with the act and continued it every time we met, much to the annoyance of The Boss. He would say, "How is my favourite girl friend?" and I would reply, "Better for seeing you." Little giggles from the children's room.

Annie wasn't just a home help, she was one of the family. I don't know if she wanted a second family as one is usually enough for anyone and she had family troubles, like everyone. Her brother, a mechanic, would come and see her for money. When she returned after her day off on a Sunday she wasn't always cheerful. My husband would call her in and tell her to have a whisky. Annie was fond of a drink and appreciated a double.

Once she was going out and I asked her where was her bag? She had her money wrapped up in a handkerchief. I told her she could not go out like that and she would bring shame to the family. I gave her money to buy bags and matching sandals as she was probably in rubber ones. She used to wear little mini dresses and she looked much younger than her years. When we went to the cinema they would think she was under age.

Janine, the French lady living near the children's school, was also a special friend. I thought it wasn't very Christian of the missionary school not to offer her a teaching job. Now I believe they must have judged her by her poor circumstances and taken it for granted that she wasn't educated. They couldn't have been more wrong. Never judge a book by its cover. When I was at boarding school we had two French teachers, one French for conversation and one English for grammar.

I should have asked them if they needed a French conversation teacher. I think they would have refused as she wasn't a "born again Christian", but nothing ventured, nothing gained. Since my return to the UK, I have written and sent photographs. Sadly, her husband replied with the sad news of her death and thanked me for the photographs.

We had another young friend, S.R. I called him that because his name was a bit of a mouthful, Shriram Katram. He was a dentist. He kindly looked after one dog Butchie (the puppy from the road) when we went to the UK for our son's wedding. He often visited us on his motorbike.

Gautam was a friend right back from Sahib's college days. He ran his own decorating business and painted our flat. We would go to a café on Marine Drive called Cream Centre, which is still there.

A couple, the Kuldip Singhs, lived in our road. He had an off-licence in Crawford Market. His wife would make me laugh – she was so direct. She once said that an Indian woman would not have stayed with my husband for more than one month.

At that time, we had two Swiss restaurants in Bombay, one in Churchgate and the other opposite Breach Candy swimming pool. Betty had a drinking problem, sadly, but they were very nice. They had one daughter and we went to her wedding.

Queenie had an English friend called Eliz Morley who was staying at the hotel. A friend of hers was an ex-head teacher called Hilda, wholived near the pool and had "Tony the Phoney" plus his boyfriend staying with her for company. Tony had originally arrived in India with the Shakespearian travelling theatre group Shakespeare Wallah and stayed on.

One Sunday morning, Eliz rang my bell and invited me over for a coffee. It was most exciting and as it all happened in such a hurry there was no time for me to decline the offer andEliz and I arrived unannounced. Tony was in a velvet jacket mixing Bloody Marys and looked very surprised to see us. Hilda came in the sitting room and Tony said, "My dear, what do you look like? Your hair!" We had a very light-hearted chat, which certainly wasn't about the price of potatoes!

Shortly after this fun morning, Tony saw me in the Taj bar and came over in his frilly lace shirt to kiss my hand. I was seven inches above the ground, Barbara Cartland lives again! Needless to say, my joy wasn't shared by my betrothed who said, "You certainly know the best people".

Family Friends

Friends of the family thought I had married for money. I told them that one didn't have to go so far to find someone rich, we had rich men in England. Didn't they think it possible for someone to love an Indian?

Talking about money, we had a house search of our flat one morning. Some jealous business opponent, I suppose, or an inquiry into the tax that the Turakhias Group of companies were paying. Each of our family members' flats were searched at the same time to prevent us warning each other. No time to hide my gold bars! The only thing I hid was my Swiss passport as having two passports was not allowed in India at that time.

A neighbour was called in to witness the amount of jewellery I had: necklace and earrings, not even a full set, with bangles and matching rings. It didn't exceed the allowed amount. I had to collect the children from school and a man came with me in case I decided to leave the country. Then my eldest brother-in-law was kidnapped. It was all very mysterious! I phoned the office about some problem I had and they told me that they didn't know where Sahib was. This wasn't unusual, so I didn't think anything strange had happened.

Ramesh, my eldest brother-in-law, had what his brother called a good heart and a bad tongue, which made it difficult to like him. He had disliked me on sight as he had intended to marry a Swiss girl, a plan that didn't materialize. Her parents didn't think he was rich enough. He was very protective, though, unlike his dear brother who was possessive but not protective. A big difference. Once, in the company bungalow in Juhu (a seaside resort in the outskirts of Bombay), a guest was being a nuisance and too attentive to my needs. Ramesh noticed this and pointed it out to my husband who told him that I could look after myself. Ramesh came to my rescue regardless, which was nice. The unwanted guest made a fast exit.

Another brother-in-law was convinced the English could not cook and when we visited him he would always ask my son if he was having bread and butter for tea. My youngest brother-in-law would help Keran, my son, with his maths and took him to cricket early in the mornings. Flowers adorned a corner in the sitting room as my brother-in-law's wife had taken a course in flower arranging. Unfortunately, their sitting room had two fridges, plastic sofas, a cabinet filled with china and funfair prizes, and bare light bulbs. It didn't offer a suitable background for a beautiful flower arrangement.

Hira, Pushba and Nila were my husband's sisters. Hira, the oldest, was gentle and kind. Pushba was a strong character and funny. I always felt safe in their homes with the protection of love. Nila, the youngest was bossy. In fact, it was Nila who spoiled my husband. They all spoiled him, but as the nearest in age to him, Nila looked after him. When I would visit her on Sundays with the children, they would send us home with a packed lunch for their naughty brother, who was just getting out of bed on our return!

My Sahib was many things but he wasn't a mouse. In nearly all the couples we knew, the men were hen-pecked. Their wives were the boss, the men were the mice. His Lordship confessed that he was a married bachelor. He was frightened of Indian women. My fault I know, I spoiled him too. Our fights were normally drink-related. When he would come home late and say, "You are not going to believe what happened to me", I would say, "Spare me the details". As long as he was safe, it was alright by me!

His so-called friends used our home like a free bar and when the whisky ran out, so did they.

Most Indian mothers spoil their sons and, had I not known my mother-in-law, I would have thought she was the reason for her three spoiled sons. The fourth and the youngest, Mukund, wasn't spoilt, contrary to general belief that the youngest is always spoilt. Ba, my mother-in-law, was very strict. I remember once when I was visiting her, the oldest son popped in and couldn't sit down as he was in too much of a hurry. She told him in no uncertain terms not to come if he didn't have the time. My command of Gujurati was not strong enough to say that, but I understood what she was saying.

Arriving home after going to the theatre with Queenie, a little surprise was waiting for me on the balcony: my husband!

"I don't think you went to the theatre, I think you met some men in the hotel," he said.

I agreed with him (the best way to avoid an argument). "Yes, we met two men. Australians, how did you guess?" I replied.

The four brothers. From the left: Bhupesh,
Ramesh, Mukund and Naresh Turakhia

Joking aside, he should have been a private detective.
He had missed his vocation even though he didn't miss
a thing. We had our telephone pad by the phone and
there were numbers in all directions on the page – it
was like a complicated map. He pointed to one number
out of the mess and asked whose number was it. I was
amazed he noticed the new number. He was a party
animal, laughed and drank, the life and soul of a party.
No villain would have been on guard with him – a big
mistake, although sometimes he couldn't see further
than his own nose. When my daughter was seventeen, I
separated from Bhupesh and returned to London. Even

though we were across continents he asked me why I told people we were separated as, in his eyes, we weren't.

The three sisters with Keran's son Sachin:
Pushba bhen, Hira bhen, and Nila behn

Spare The Rod

The biblical saying, "Spare the rod and spoil the child" comes to mind. I have always been heavy-handed and once I lose my temper, I'm out of control.

My mother told me that whenever this happens I should lock myself in a room to cool off. She said if I lost it with my husband it wasn't dangerous as he was stronger than I was, but the children weren't. This advice stayed with me and one day when I was out of my comfort zone, like every morning with the heat, the children, who were about eight and ten, were arguing between themselves.

"Oh yes you were!"
"Oh no I wasn't!"
"Oh yes..."

You know the routine. I thought my head would burst. They were walking behind me in the hall. I pushed them over and they fell in a heap and I locked myself in the kitchen. I never hit them again.

Colour

Some Indian people are very colour-conscious, which resulted in ladies going to the hairdressers to have their face and arms bleached. When I was there, to be fair was more important than to be beautiful. Wedding videos usually included a few light-skinned foreigners as a status symbol.

Indian men who married Americans would return to India on holiday on Cloud Nine and behaving like the Lord of the Manor.

In the swimming pool, we were all colour-blind. The darker skinned females wore black, navy or brown while the whites wore near white, yellow or pale pink.

Mixed marriages are strange, as some of their offspring look white European, some Indian and others look between the two, perhaps like Spanish or Italians.

How lovely to be born with a beautiful tan!

Family and nearly family

My husband did not like my friends and Queenie no exception. The reasons were:

1. She had a profession
2. Her husband was a very good dancer

He taught his three daughters to jive. We couldn't manage to teach one daughter, let alone three. I would often go to their home for family gatherings and parties – I love Goan food. Crystal, the oldest, was into computers and was a cool seamstress. Sunshine was an air-hostess for a time. She was on a hijacked plane along with my German friend Margaret. Margaret said Sunshine handled her job so well and was very brave and calm. Pearl, the baby, was into sport and cycled many mornings. They were looked after by their Grandma, as Queenie, who they called "Darling", was at work all day. The first time Gran heard the two of us being rude to each other she was most upset. Queenie had to explain that we did it all the time – it's what friends do. Outsiders overhearing us also got the wrong end of the stick. We were just misunderstood.

Back in the Turakhia household, I never knew if my eldest brother-in-law's wife was allergic to "Namaste" (Greetings) or allergic to me, for as soon as she saw me she would quickly turn and I was left paying my respects to her back!

Peshna did a correspondence course with Wolsey Hall, taking her GCEs before going to the UK.

When Peshna and I left Bombay, it was under the pretext of buying a home, which didn't materialise. We stayed with my ex-neighbour from Juhu. She had remarried and lived in Thornton Heath. My mother's flat was very small and I stayed in a long term let in Gloucester Road for a time. It was owned by a property company and was run by a manageress who was half-Russian and half-Irish. What a combination! Needless to say, we got on very well.

Some time after I returned to India, we had a blast from the past. My daughter, without prior warning, turned up in India with a friend called Helen. They did not tell us they were coming but went straight to the Sun-n-Sand in Juhu, the hotel that Queenie had business interests in. We were told of their arrival through Queenie. When they eventually visited us, the two advised me that I should go visit a psychiatrist the next time I was in England. Trying shock tactics, I told them I would get a boyfriend – but you know what they say: be careful what you wish for.

Keran went to boarding school at Sevenoaks School. As luck would have it, the headmaster was experimenting with a new concept which involved housing the international students separately in the International Center. Our friend did not like the idea but my son did. He was used to mixing with different nationalities from his boarding school in Ooty. At an Open Day

Queenie and Anna Turakhia in the Shalimar Hotel.

I talked to their matron who said that during the first term they were very naughty but afterwards had settled down. It seems they achieved very high grades, much to the head's delight. His idea had paid off.

When I phoned the dormitory, the students thought I was Keran's girlfriend and would queue up to talk to me. A real madhouse!

Anna Bhupesh and Annie, our home help,
with Caroline, Keran's girlfriend and future wife

Bad Friends

Jenny and I had been to our pavement club to feed the poor children. It was very depressing, so we decided afterwards to go to the Cricket Club of India (the CCI) for a few drinks and dinner.

We rang my husband and asked him to join us. "No," was the sharp response. A chap there who used to play bridge with Joan's late husband joined us for a coffee. It was all quite pleasant, but our second cup of coffee had tasted rather odd. Making a quick exit, we left with a hasty farewell. It seemed that this member had a habit of spiking people's drinks. The next morning I was amazed to see how well the car was parked; despite me blacking out and not being able to remember a thing, I had been able to drive home and park the car in our difficult space without any problems at all.

Some "friends" should come with a warning sign on their forehead; a case of "beware of friends" and not "beware of strangers". The bad side of clubs, I suppose, is feeling too safe. Maybe the card player didn't just play with cards.

Here I Go Again

Back in London and staying with my mother, I found a job. It was a relief. I was a manageress for Holiday Lets, a short-term letting company. There were six houses with six managers and I stood in as the floating manageress. I covered any of the houses when the main manager could not be there.

It was a live-in job and I had a nice little office where I supervised the daily morning maids, answered the phone and took bookings. I was there for about two years before I returned to Bombay, to my homeless husband. He was staying in the CCI as he had sold our flat to finance my move to England with my daughter's and my son's private A-level education.

There was a charming bachelor we met in the bar. He was the first Indian to go to Harvard University and had owned race horses in the past. My boss told him he shouldn't strain his eyes; he was screwing up his forehead. He answered that he would strain his eyes to look at me but not to look at him. That didn't go down very well, as you can imagine. The following evening I was confined to quarters.

I would ask him the meaning of different random long words. "No one will understand you if you use them", he would say. "That's the idea" I would reply. While we were still at the CCI, my son's then girlfriend, Caroline, and her sister Helen came to visit India. Helen was going to Cambridge University at the end of the year. They toured India on a shoe-string budget, travelling third class on the trains. Really brave in India. Remember there were no mobile phones then. They visited some friends of ours in Delhi but after that they were on their own. In those days, girls without an escort/ brother/uncle were considered cheap, certainly not from a good family.

Despite my worries, it all ended well and they returned unharmed. We had moved to our new home and missed the luxury of the club. Who wants a home with all that? Our humble little flat in the suburbs of Mumbai did not feel a fair exchange.

Memories Are Made Of This

I remember my three-year-old daughter being so happy when Bapuji admired her button necklace. He valued what the one he loved valued. In India, servant girls usually wear 22 carat gold chains. We should be more like children. Being poor isn't always sad and wealth can't buy happiness. I have a picture my daughter drew at the age of four. The flowers are taller than the house. Values are more important than facts: something living next to something dead.

Diamonds To Ashes

After Kailas, our flat in the centre of Bombay, our first move was to Kurla, a fairly affluent suburb near Chembur. We were in a small block with three flats per floor on the wrong side of the street. The good thing about our flat was the mixed community. Everyone was so friendly. We became very friendly with Goans on the ground floor – a beautiful family. Then there were Hindus, Maharashtrians and more.

The bad thing was that it was a compound; I don't like compounds. The vegetable wallahs (hawkers) came daily, which was a great help as having to buy your vegetables in the market and come back in a rickshaw would have been difficult. This is where we acquired Butchie, our puppy with the rat bite.

I invited a few children to tea. It was a flop as I gave them egg and tomato sandwiches which they didn't eat.

Margaret, my friend from Bombay, would visit me. Her husband would drop her off on his way to a nearby factory. Wasn't that sweet? She would spend the day with me. She is class like my youngest brother-in-law

Mukund's wife, Duksha. Her father spoke fluent French (not school French) and I was most impressed. We would have invited him to our French coffee parties, but it was ladies only.

We eventually had to move as the flat belonged to a friend who wanted it back. We moved to Panvel. Talk about jumping out of the frying pan and into a fire. This wasn't a flat but a semi-detached house also in a compound. All the residents were Gujuratis, like my family, but they couldn't have been more different. The family had accepted me and couldn't have been kinder. These neighbours were hostile. Some people will not accept change. It isn't only an Eastern problem: the amateur drama group that I tried to perform for were just the same. Small place, small minds – no outsiders welcome. I was most unhappy. Something that should have been fun was a nightmare. After attending my friend's husband's funeral, I surprised my husband with some home truths. My friend was Swiss and her late husband an affluent member of the Indian society. I told my husband that if he died first I would never stay on.

It was then that he decided to make future plans for me to live in the UK. He said he would join me but I knew he would never leave India. The children were already in England so the die was cast. Once it was all settled, he lost interest. He slept downstairs with the dog and I had a room upstairs. I felt disowned. Once away, I stayed with my son and daughter-in-law, living in a flat nearby before renting one.

My husband would come on holidays. He had actually booked a return ticket to Bombay when he suddenly succumbed to cancer. It was very quick, fortunately.

Morning Madness

The chaotic mornings are the first thing my son remembers when we talk about India. Every morning, the doorbell would ring continuously. The dog would bark whenever the doorbell rang, then the phone would ring! Hawkers were forbidden but managed to slip by the watchman. We had vegetable wallahs (hawkers), fruit wallahs, post, even buyers who were offering to pay for our old papers and bottles. The milkman came twice, the first time to deliver milk and collect money, then later to deliver milk, hours after queuing at the milk delivery van. Regarding the phone, I can't think how we had so many calls as cold calls didn't exist then. Sweet mysteries of life. I will never know.

Bhupesh with Butchie our dog in Panvel,
the down-sized house, after a lot of adversity

Once Upon A Murder

On Annie's first day working as our nanny, we experienced the most horrific ordeal. My mother-in-law was murdered.

One of her sons was about to be married and a set of Indian-style jewellery lay in the cupboard – the reason for the assault.

While Ba, my husband's mother, was praying in her usual morning practice, she was stabbed several times. She then walked to the lift and asked shocked onlookers for her husband and son to be called. Her wishes were met; she always wanted to die in her husband's arms with her eldest son by her side.

The temporary servant was caught. A young man hiding in the basement. We know Ba would not have wished him any harm. I was honoured to be asked to say a few words at the funeral of a guardian angel for me, and a person who valued and respected life so much.

My husband took a shower by the side of the pool, fully dressed, hoping, no doubt, to wash away the angst and pain.

Epilogue

You might be wondering why I called this book *How Do You Pass Your Time?* It was a question Indian memsahibs constantly asked me. I'm sure they didn't ask Indian women the same question. What was the mystery surrounding me? "Have you a servant?" I would ask them. "Yes" was the answer. "Well, ask him what he does – that's what I do!"

Final plea. Adding "bhai" (brother) and "bhen" (sister) to given names is a sign of respect. I have omitted these, but no lack of admiration was intended. I hope at my great age it longer applies and that it allows me to waive the rules.

Please remember that this all took place a long time ago. Many things have changed, no doubt. February 1963, to be exact, was when it started.

Printed in Great Britain
by Amazon